30 Days of Chakra Balancing

Your Own Personal Chakra Journey for Learning and Navigating the Chakric System for Love, Health, Wealth and Happiness and More

Diana Loera

Copyright 2022 All rights reserved

Without limiting the rights under the copyright reserved above, no part of this book may be reproduced, stored in or introduced into a retrieval system, or transmitted, in any form, or by any means (electronic, mechanical, photocopying, recording, or otherwise) without the prior written permission of Diana Loera and Loera Publishing LLC.

Book piracy and any other forms of unauthorized distribution or use without written permission by Diana Loera/Loera Publishing LLC will be prosecuted to the fullest extent of the law.

Table of Contents

Other Books Available From Loera Publishing LLC 5
Introduction 6
The Origin of the Word Chakra 7
The Benefits of Chakra Balancing 8
The Importance of Chakra Balancing 9
A Walk Through the Chakras 10
   1. Root Chakra 10
   2. Sacral Chakra 10
   3. Solar Plexus Chakra 10
   4. Heart Chakra 10
   5. Throat Chakra 11
   6. Third Eye Chakra 11
   7. Crown Chakra 11
   History of the Chakra System 12
   Chakra Chart 13
   Chakras and Colors 14
   The Root Chakra Color Red 14
   The Sacral Chakra Color Orange 14
   The Solar Plexus Chakra Color Yellow 15
   The Heart Chakra Color Green 15
   The Throat Chakra Color Blue 16
   Third Eye Chakra Color Indigo 16
   Crown Chakra Color White 17
   Summary of The Chakras 18
   Powerful Affirmations for Chakra Balancing 19
   Second Set Powerful Affirmations for Chakra Balancing 20
   Chakra Meditation Scripts 21
   The Root Chakra (Mooladhara Chakra) 22
   Chakra Meditation Script Chakra One Root Chakra 23
   The Sacral Chakra (Swadhisthana Chakra) 24
   Chakra Meditation Script Chakra Two Sacral Chakra 25
   The Solar Plexus Chakra (Manipura Chakra) 26

Chakra Meditation Script Chakra Three Solar Plexus Chakra 26
The Heart Chakra (Anahata Chakra) 27
Chakra Meditation Script Chakra Four Heart Chakra 27
The Throat Chakra (Vishuddhi Chakra) 29
Chakra Meditation Script Chakra Five Throat Chakra 29
The Third Eye Chakra (Ajna Chakra) 30
Chakra Meditation Script Chakra Six Third Eye Chakra 30
The Crown Chakra (Sahasrara Chakra) 32
Chakra Meditation Script Chakra Seven Crown Chakra 32
30 Day Chakra Journey Workbook 34

Other Books Available From Loera Publishing LLC

Available in bookstores everywhere. Over 600 books in print including:

Tarot Card Reader 3 Card Spread Journal Logbook: 3 Card Tarot Spread Tracker, Logbook, Journal

A Year of Tarot Card Reading: 12 Monthly & 52 Weekly Guides for the Tarot Card Reader

Tarot Cards Coloring and Learning Workbook: Mastering Tarot Card Meaning and Symbols

Tarot Card Workbook Journal: A Personal Learning Tarot Card Workbook Journal for Understanding and Reading Tarot Cards

Rune Casting Workbook: Learning Guide for Reading Runes

Introduction

In this book, we'll be learning how you can tap into your chakra system and ultimately improve your life in many or all areas – better sleep, better sex, less stress, more peace, increased wealth and much more to make your life better.

We'll go through each of the seven main chakras:

What a chakra is

What characteristics each of the seven chakras have

Affirmations for each chakra

Balancing each chakra

Meditation

You'll then do a 30-day chakra journey that will become your own unique experience

The Origin of the Word Chakra

The word chakra steams from Sanskrit. Sanskrit is the root of many, but not all Indian languages.

If you know Sanskrit, you understand and converse in many Indian languages such as Hindi, Bengali and Marathi

Chakra means circle or wheel.

The Benefits of Chakra Balancing

Chakra Balancing is a form of energy healing that focuses on channeling energy into the seven chakras.

When we talk about balancing our chakras, we're referring to treating our energetic body.

The body is not only made up of the physical body, we have an energy that extends beyond our physical self.

The chakras we will be focusing on in this book are the ones we tend to consider as the seven main ones of the body.

The aim is to release any chakra blockages and promote a free flow of energy to restore balance and a sense of wellbeing.

When chakras are balanced and running in harmony, you may feel improvements such as less stress, feeling peaceful, more calm and focused.

The Importance of Chakra Balancing

As you progress through this book and workbook, you'll become more fully aware of each of the seven chakras, their respective colors and the organs that they impact.

You'll learn about the improvements that will occur in your body and life as you awaken and balance the seven main chakras.

Balanced chakras create a harmonious balance within your life as the seven chakras become and stay balanced.

A Walk Through the Chakras

Let's take a walk and look at each of these main seven chakras one by one. It may be helpful for you to touch the area where this chakra may have an energy point to help increase your familiarity with the location today.

1. Root Chakra – Sits at the base of your spine or tailbone.

Physical imbalances manifest themselves as problems in the legs, rectum, tailbone, immune system, male reproductive parts and prostate gland.

Emotional imbalances manifest themselves as feelings affecting the basic survival needs; money, shelter, food and the ability to provide life's necessities.

2. Sacral Chakra – Two inches below your navel

Physical imbalances manifest themselves as sexual and reproductive issues, urinary problems, kidney infections, hip pelvic and lower back pain.

Emotional imbalances manifest themselves as fear of commitment to relationships, expressing emotions, fears of impotence, betrayal and addictions.

3. Solar Plexus Chakra – Three inches above your navel

Physical imbalances manifest themselves as digestive problems, liver dysfunction, chronic fatigue, high blood pressure, diabetes, stomach ulcers and colon issues.

Emotional imbalances manifest themselves as issues of personal power and self-esteem.

4. Heart Chakra – at the heart

Physical imbalances manifest themselves as asthma, heart disease, lung disease, issues with breasts, lymphatic systems and upper back and shoulder problems.

Emotional imbalances manifest themselves as jealousy, abandonment, anger, bitterness and fear of loneliness.

5. Throat Chakra – at the throat

Physical imbalances manifest themselves as thyroid issues, sore throats, laryngitis, ear infections, neck and shoulder pain.

Emotional imbalances manifest themselves as fear of communication, will-power and being out of control.

6. Third Eye Chakra – in the middle of the eyebrows

Physical imbalances manifest themselves as headaches, blurred vision, sinus issues, seizures, hearing loss and hormonal imbalance.

Emotional imbalances manifest themselves as moodiness, volatility and self-reflection.

7. Crown Chakra – top of the head

Physical imbalances manifest themselves as depression, inability to learn, sensitivity to light, sound and the environment.

Emotional imbalances manifest themselves as confusion, prejudice and self-doubt.

History of the Chakra System

The chakra system originated in India between 1500 and 500 BC. You will find it mentioned in the oldest text called the Vedas.

Evidence of chakras, spelled cakra, is also found in the Shri Jabala Darshana Upanishad, the Cudamini Upanishad, the Yogashikha Upanishad and the Shandilya Upanishad.

Chakra Chart

Chakras and Colors

Each of the seven chakras carries a specific meaning and color.

In this chapter, we'll cover the significance of all the seven chakras, their colors, and the areas of our health and life these chakras tend to influence.

The Root Chakra Color Red

In Sanskrit, the Root Chakra is known as the Muladhara Chakra; this chakra defines our relationship with Mother Earth.

It influences our passion, creativity, youthfulness, vitality and most importantly, our basic survival instincts.

The Root Chakra is represented by the color red, which is also an indication for the need of logic, realistic thinking and order in our lives.

It is also symbolic of our physical strength, our sexuality and the flight and fight response that tends to activate within our body when we sense danger.

The Root Chakra is connected with the sense of smell within the body, and it is attached to the gland known as Gonads.

The Sacral Chakra Color Orange

The Sacral Chakra, or the Svadhisthana Chakra, is symbolic of the water elements present within the human body. It is represented by the color orange, which tends to impact our ability to be happy and joyful, compassionate, creative and passionate.

It also influences our desires, sexuality and our reproductive functions amongst others.

Within the human body, the Sacral Chakra is connected with our sense of taste, and it impacts several organs and glands, including the bladder, the lymphatic system, pelvis, the large intestine and the female reproductive organs.

The Solar Plexus Chakra Color Yellow

The Solar Plexus Chakra, known as the Manipura Chakra in Sanskrit. The word Manipura is roughly translated to City of Jewels.

This chakra is regarded as one of the most powerful chakras that has profound influences on our personal power. The Solar Plexus chakra represents our personal abilities and powers, and it influences both our personal and professional success.

The Solar Plexus chakra is represented by the color yellow.

Yellow definitely symbolizes the energy vortex and its connection with energy and fire and powerful emotions. When this chakra is operating as it should and is balanced it helps us to be more energetic, active, confident and cheerful. It helps with self-confidence and self-esteem.

The Solar Plexus chakra is connected to our sense of sight, and with the adrenal glands.

The Heart Chakra Color Green

The Heart Chakra, also known as the Anahata Chakra has the most impact on our personal as well as professional relationships in this life.

This chakra is associated with the element Air within the body.

Green is the color we associate with this chakra. If this chakra is not balanced, one may have relationship issues such as anger, distrust and jealousy.

The Heart Chakra is tied to our sense of touch. It is connected to several glands, including the lymph and thymus glands.

The Throat Chakra Color Blue

The Vishuddhi Chakra (or Throat Chakra) is represented by the color blue.

This chakra symbolizes our true inner voice and communication with others including listening and empathizing.

When the Throat Chakra is balanced, it allows us to enjoy creative expression, artistic potential, utilize our energy in the best possible way and the ability to reach a higher spiritual awareness.

This chakra is connected to the throat, neck, jaws, ears, teeth, esophagus, and thyroid.

Third Eye Chakra Color Indigo

The Third Eye Chakra (sometimes called the Brow Chakra) is also known is the Ajna Chakra. Ajna translates roughly to the center of knowledge. This chakra is symbolized by the color indigo.

This chakra is associated with the way we think, rationalize, analyze and use logic.

An individual with a balanced Third Eye Chakra, tends to be very charismatic. They also tend to be highly intuitive and possibly telepathic.

This chakra relates to various glands including the pineal gland and pituitary gland.

Crown Chakra Color White

The top chakra of the seven, known as the Sahasrara Chakra in Sanskrit, is connected with the element of light.

It is associated with several organs and glands within the body, including the brain, the hands, the nervous system, and the pituitary gland.

When this chakra is harmoniously balanced, it can provide individuals with some extremely powerful abilities and potentials, including the ability to transcend all barriers created by the laws of nature, to possess an increased awareness of death and immortality, heightened spiritual powers and even the ability to create miracles.

Summary of The Chakras

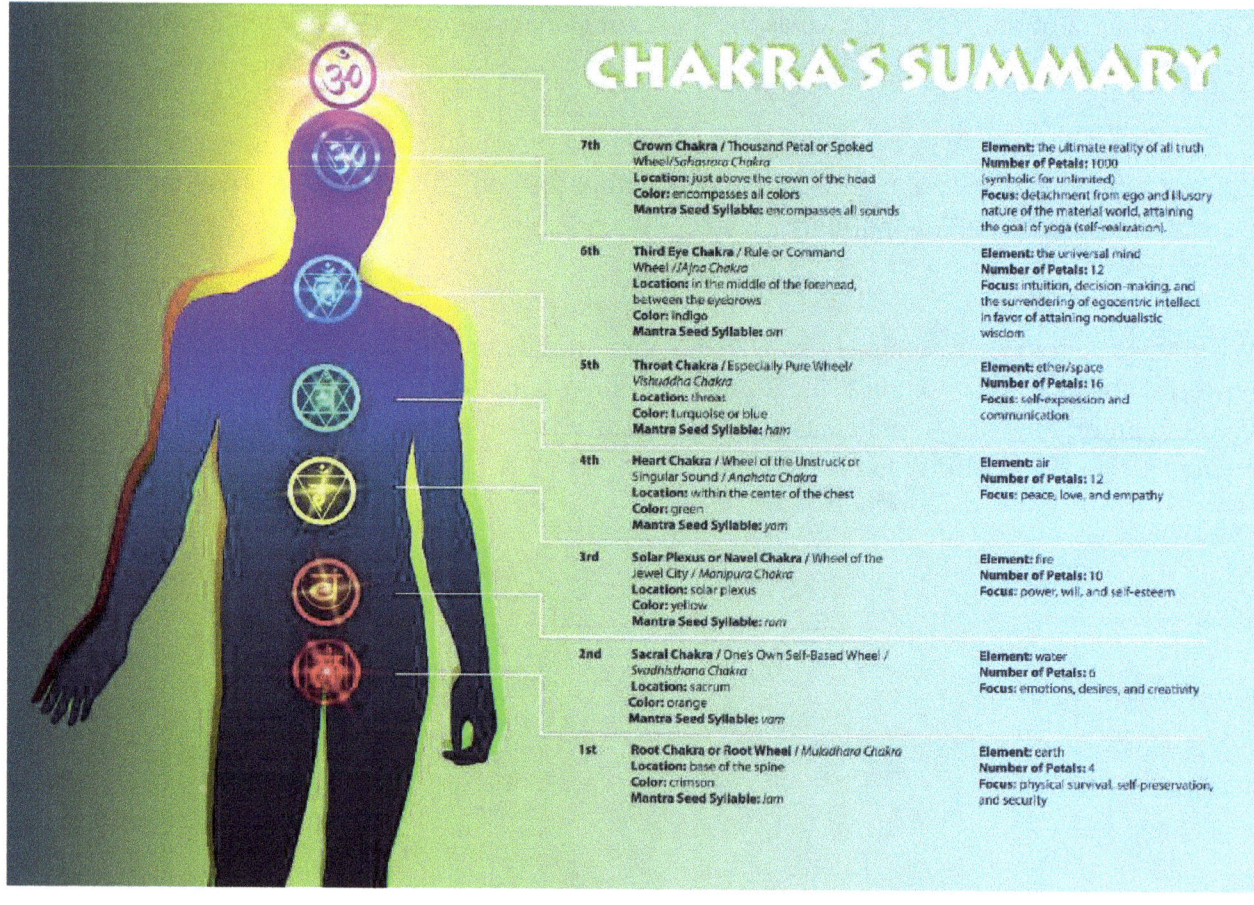

Powerful Affirmations for Chakra Balancing

Our seven chakras are responsible for the flow of energy through the body. When they are open and aligned, we can more easily bring forward power, love, and inner wisdom to everything we do. When the chakras are blocked, though, it can lead to physical and mental stagnation.

It is by aligning with our chakras that we get to acknowledge and embrace all aspects of ourselves.

By using affirmations to bring our chakras into balance, we are acknowledging that we are filled with greatness (Crown Chakra) and filled with humility (Root Chakra). We are acknowledging that we are learning and growing (Throat Chakra), and we are working to accept and embrace our strengths and weaknesses (Solar Plexus).

Crown Chakra: I am filled with greatness.

Third-Eye Chakra: I am wise.

Throat Chakra: I am learning, and I am growing. We are all learning and growing.

Heart Chakra: I love and appreciate myself as I am.

Solar Plexus Chakra: I accept myself completely. I accept that I have strengths, and I accept that I have weaknesses.

Sacral Chakra: I am both sensitive and strong.

Root Chakra: I am filled with humility. I am enough as I am.

Second Set Powerful Affirmations for Chakra Balancing

Chakra balancing is a very important tool for tapping into your most authentic self. Below is one more set of affirmations.

Experience the power, confidence, and strength that comes from balancing and aligning all of your chakra. See and feel the transformation that occurs in your body and life.

Crown Chakra: I let go, and I trust the process of life.

Third-Eye Chakra: I am a wise decision-maker.

Throat Chakra: I am filled with the power of spirit.

Heart Chakra: I am filled with courage.

Solar Plexus Chakra: I accept that I am learning and growing.

Sacral Chakra: I am balanced. I know when to act, and I know when to wait.

Root Chakra: I am disciplined.

Chakra Meditation Scripts

For some, meditation can be a really easy practice to get into with no one to guide them. But not everyone has this ease, some may prefer a guided path and that is totally fine.

In this chapter, you'll find more information on each chakra as well as a guided meditation script as an example. You can record a script, have a friend or family member record it or look online for a guided recorded script.

If you choose to record a script, the ones in this chapter should take around five to seven minutes to record.

These scripts will be focusing on healing and restoring the seven main chakras.

Since each chakra is associated with a particular aspect of our lives, we will be focusing on those as well in these meditations.

You can use the following script for all chakras at the beginning of each recording or you can use it once and continue on to record each chakra section.

To begin our meditation, sit down on a hard level surface. If you find the floor is too uncomfortable, you may use a mat or pillow to sit on. Sit up straight and rest your hands gently in your lap.

The Root Chakra (Mooladhara Chakra)

A blocked root chakra is generally related to stress, often involving career worries and financial dependence (or independence, accordingly). Often, people with a blocked root chakra are very concerned regarding their emotional or physical wellbeing.

Symptoms of a blocked root chakra includes pelvic or lower back pain, as well as cold extremities and trouble concentrating.

Chakra Meditation Script Chakra One Root Chakra

As you sit down, feel the ground rise up to catch and support you. Feel yourself grounded in the earth and watch your worries wash away. You're here now, you're alive and you're cared for. You're protected.

Allow your eyes to close gently as the waves of your worries grow still and subside. Calm waters. Eyes closed. You are safe. Take a deep, long breath. Feel it in every inch of your body. Visualize your breath as it travels through your nose, down your throat and into your lungs. Feel your chest expand as the breath filters through your lungs. Feel the air go down into your belly, your pelvic bone and thighs. Let your things grow heavy and your spine to ground.

Continuing to breathe, travel down with your breath. Visualize your journey. Throat, lungs, belly, lower back and into the spine. Focus on the end of your tailbone and see your root chakra. The bright, red chakra staring back at you. Watch as the red light grows larger, expands across your lower back. The red light is warm and soothing.

Feel the red light, like a supportive hand on your lower back. Let the red light spread across your lower back and heal. Ground down into your root chakra and rise up slowly from the base of your spine.

Travel upwards with that healing, red light. Open your eyes and feel the light wash through your body. Outside, nothing has happened. Inside you, your root chakra glows.

The Sacral Chakra (Svadhisthana Chakra)

The Sacral Chakra is closely intertwined with our pleasure center, our overall satisfaction and sexuality. A blocked Sacral Chakra can also signify difficulties accepting new people or experiences into our lives.

Symptoms of a blocked Sacral Chakra manifests primarily in the reproductive organs, the kidneys and the bowels.

Chakra Meditation Script Chakra Two Sacral Chakra

Close your eyes and allow the earth to rise up to catch you. Feel yourself in the present moment and know that you're loved and supported. Visualize in your mind the stillness of the earth, the perfectly smooth line that you are sitting on. Let that line become your horizon and your freedom. At this moment, you are free.

Slowly, with your eyes closed, begin to visualize a large orange right below your navel. Sweet or sour. Imagine the delicious juice inside this orange. Imagine the taste filling your mouth. Let the orange grow and the details grow blurry. You can no longer see the orange clearly any longer.

Instead, you watch as the bright color slowly dissipates into an ocean, turning the light waves orange and bright, like the sun.

Watch as this ocean gently spreads out through your body. Feel the waves run down your thighs, into your calves and all the way down to your toes. Watch as the gust of water rushes up your spine and begins to fill every inch of skin, runs down your arms, fingers and up, all the way to the head. Feel the sweet taste of the water once more flood your mouth.

The water flows warm. The waves have your back. You are free like the ocean within you.

You are free.

You are free.

The Solar Plexus Chakra (Manipura Chakra)

A blocked Solar Plexus Chakra signifies a lack of control and confidence. Often enough, when our Solar Plexus Chakra is blocked, we begin to doubt our worth, opinions and achievements.

As this chakra is located in the stomach area, it can manifest the blockage with ssues with the liver, pancreas, digestive tract or even skin outbreaks.

Chakra Meditation Script Chakra Three Solar Plexus Chakra

Close your eyes and feel your lower limbs grow heavy and still until you can no longer distinguish between them and the earth you're sitting on. Instead, turn your attention to the bright, yellow flame in your solar plexus, right beneath your ribcage. Your epicenter. Visualize your inner sun and see it burst into flames.

What you see is your passion, your center, your inner fire. As the fire grows, so does your power. Like a lion, your teeth grow sharp and bold as the fire within you spreads. Like an eagle, you begin to soar in the sky, high above this earth that only a moment ago grounded you and held you captive. Visualize yourself breaking free, see yourself tearing your body and spreading your wings.

Feel the power flood your every pore as you glide through the sky. You are an eagle and a lion, all wrapped up in one. Feel the mighty roar rise up within you. You are strong. On the count of three, you will let out this roar.

One…

Two…

Three…

The Heart Chakra (Anahata Chakra)

A blocked Heart Chakra is reflected in the people you surround yourself with. You may unknowingly seek out toxic relationships or even push people away from you. Your Heart Chakra is closely associated with your ability to love and feel empathy.

Physically, your Heart Chakra is situated near the heart, but can manifest itself as problems with the immune system, the respiratory and circulatory system also.

Chakra Meditation Script Chakra Four Heart Chakra

Bring your attention to your breathing. Focus and visualize the air coming in and out of your lungs. Slowly, expand your breaths so that each time, you take in a little more.

Breathe in through the nose, out through the mouth. In through the nose, out through the mouth.

As you do this, feel your body relax. Feel your limbs grow heavy and grounded as you breathe.

Visualize the ground and notice a bright ball of green energy at the very base of your spine. Emerald-green, this ball is the most beautiful jewel you have ever seen. Like a child, you reach out your hand and gently wrap your fingers around the green ball. As slowly as you possibly can, begin dragging the ball up along your spine and towards your heart. This jewel is for your heart.

As you rise up along the spine, repeat to yourself this affirmation:

'I do not take this jewel out of jealousy, for I am generous. I do not take this jewel for myself, because I am loved. I take this jewel for my family and friends, because it will delight them as it delights me. I am loved and this jewel proves it.'

Repeat this to yourself and each time, take the jewel a little higher along your body, until you reach the heart.

'I do not take this jewel out of jealousy, for I am generous. I do not take this jewel for myself, because I am loved. I take this jewel for my family and friends, because it will delight them as it delights me. I am loved and this jewel proves it.'

When the jewel has reached your heart, bring your focus back to your breath. With each breath, see the jewel grow a little bigger. With each exhale, watch it become a little brighter. You are growing this jewel so that everyone in your life can have a little. Your friends, your family. Everyone.

Breathe in. breathe out. Watch the jewel expand.

The Throat Chakra (Vishuddhi Chakra)

A blocked Throat Chakra manifests itself through an inability to speak. If you have trouble expressing your thoughts or conveying your feelings, then your Throat Chakra might be in trouble. Alternatively, if you're weighed down by a secret, your Throat Chakra can become blocked.

Problems in the Throat Chakra show up in the throat, vocal chords, teeth, thyroid and respiratory system.

Chakra Meditation Script Chakra Five Throat Chakra

To open your Throat Chakra, you'll need a lot of air.

Opening up your Throat Chakra is easy. You simply need to breathe in and out.

Breathe in through your nose and out through your mouth.

In and out.

Take ten deep, long breaths.

Count them in your mind.

In, out.

[Pause]

In, out. When your lungs have become filled with air, begin slowly going down through your body, starting from the top of your head. As you go, imagine each muscle relax and let go. Let go.

Let go in your mouth. Let go in your throat. Let go in your chest. Let go in your belly. Let go in your hips. Let go in your thighs. Let go. Once your entire body has relaxed, slowly travel back up to your throat. Visualize your Throat Chakra. You see a blue spinning ball at throat level. As the ball spins, you see it glowing and expanding. The ball grows and spins faster and faster. It draws energy. All the energy that you were holding in your muscles has gone into this blue ball.

Bright blue ball.

The more the ball grows, the more relaxation you feel in your throat. The more you can breathe in. When the ball grows too big for you to hold on to, let go. Feel all the pent-up energy inside that ball expand and flow through your body. You can now open your eyes. You can now breathe.

The Third Eye Chakra (Ajna Chakra)

The Third Eye Chakra is rooted in your thinking mind and sense of being. A blocked Third Eye Chakra manifests itself in feelings of pointlessness, lack of direction and even paranoia.

Physically, you may experience headaches and sinus pain.

Chakra Meditation Script Chakra Six Third Eye Chakra

Bring your attention to the top of your head. As you sit, feel your forehead grow light and your thinking mind fall quiet. Let any worries and thoughts fall silent, as you slowly breathe in through the nose and out through the mouth. As your lungs become filled with air, your body slowly begins to relax, starting from your head all the way to your toes. Feel your lower body grow heavy and your upper body grow light as a feather.

Feel the freedom and the air flow through your limbs and all the way into your forehead. Feel your forehead grow cool and weightless. Slowly, as you rid yourself of all thoughts and worries, begin to visualize a small purple ball at the centre of your forehead. This is your Third Eye. as your two normal eyes are closed and sightless, your Third Eye begins to expand and grow, accumulating more and more energy as it goes.

See this purple ball glow and grow larger, but not heavier. Your Third Eye is also light as a feather. As the purple ball begins to push against the edges of your forehead, feel it push against them and then burst open. Imagine the purple energy of your Third Eye flowing freely through your body. Head, throat, chest, belly and legs, feel them all drenched in this wonderful purple energy.

As you open your eyes, feel your Third Eye light and heal.

The Crown Chakra (Sahasrara Chakra)

The Crown Chakra is directly connected with how much beauty you can see in the world around you. A blocked Crown Chakra can manifest through feelings of stress and being overwhelmed.

Exhaustion, headaches and sleepiness are the most common symptoms of a blocked Crown Chakra.

Chakra Meditation Script Chakra Seven Crown Chakra

As you feel your body relax, you begin to picture a beautiful flower bud on the top of your head. Breathe slowly and with each breath, begin to see this flower a little clearer. It is a baby flower. Breathe. It is a lotus flower, but it is closed. Continue breathing. In through the nose and out through the mouth.

As your breath grows deeper and steadier, you notice the lotus flower on the top of your head begin to bloom and open. Breathe. See the petals expanding and the lotus flower begin to shine. As you breathe, a dim violet light begins to shine through the lotus. See that with each breath, the violet light becomes a little brighter. And a little more. Until the whole room becomes bathed in violet light and the crown of your head can barely contain it. You will take three more breaths and then release the violet light.

Breathe in. Breathe out.

Breathe in. Breathe out.

Breathe in. Breathe out.

Now let go. See the bright violet light flow through your body and the lotus flower sit majestically atop your head. You are healed. Open your eyes and see the world through this warm violet light.

You can practice chakra meditation when you feel stress, but you can also do them when you're feeling fine, to boost the wellbeing of your chakras. Balanced and opened chakras allow us to lead a happy, balanced and open life.

30 Day Chakra Journey Workbook

Following is your 30-Day Chakra Journey Workbook.

There are no right or wrong answers – this is your personal journey.

You can use this section solely as a chakra workbook or expand upon it and incorporate it into your daily life as a planner. This is your choice – make this section as unique as you are.

30 Days of Chakra Learning Workbook

MONTH:

MON	TUES	WED	THURS	FRI	SAT	SUN

GOAL TRACKER

GOAL _____

1	2	3	4	5	6	7

8	9	10	11	12	13	14

15	16	17	18	19	20	21

22	23	24	25	26	27	28

29	30	31				

WEEK OF:

MON	TUES
WED	THURS
FRI	SAT
SUN	NOTES

TO DO: _____

MON
- ○ _____
- ○ _____
- ○ _____
- ○ _____

TUES
- ○ _____
- ○ _____
- ○ _____
- ○ _____

WED
- ○ _____
- ○ _____
- ○ _____
- ○ _____

THURS
- ○ _____
- ○ _____
- ○ _____
- ○ _____

FRI
- ○ _____
- ○ _____
- ○ _____
- ○ _____

SAT
- ○ _____
- ○ _____
- ○ _____
- ○ _____

SUN
- ○ _____
- ○ _____
- ○ _____
- ○ _____

NOTES
- ○ _____
- ○ _____
- ○ _____
- ○ _____

1-MINUTE REFLECTIONS

MON

TUES

WED

THURS

FRI

SAT

SUN

NOTES

MONDAY:

ROOT CHAKRA:

TO-DO
_____
_____
_____
_____

AFFIRMATION

SCHEDULE
_____
_____
_____
_____
_____
_____
_____
_____
_____
_____
_____
_____
_____
_____
_____
_____
_____
_____

APPOINTMENTS

TO-DO
_____
_____
_____
_____
_____
_____
_____
_____
_____
_____

MOOD

MONDAY:

ROOT CHAKRA:

TO-DO

AFFIRMATION

SCHEDULE

APPOINTMENTS

TO-DO

MOOD

TUESDAY:

SACRAL CHAKRA:

TO-DO

AFFIRMATION

SCHEDULE

APPOINTMENTS

TO-DO

MOOD

TUESDAY:

SACRAL CHAKRA:

AFFIRMATION:

GOALS	AM	PM	MEALS
○ ○ ○			BREAKFAST LUNCH DINNER SNACKS WATER 💧💧💧💧💧💧💧💧 EXERCISE

| GRATITUDE

 CHAKRA CARE | TO DO
 ○
 ○
 ○
 ○
 ○
 ○
 ○
 ○
 ○
 ○ | NOTES |

WEDNESDAY:

POWER CENTER:

TO-DO

SCHEDULE

AFFIRMATION

APPOINTMENTS

TO-DO

MOOD

WEDNESDAY:

POWER CENTER:

AFFIRMATION:

GOALS	AM	PM	MEALS
○ ○ ○			BREAKFAST / LUNCH / DINNER / SNACKS / WATER / EXERCISE

GRATITUDE

CHAKRA CARE

TO DO
- ○
- ○
- ○
- ○
- ○
- ○
- ○
- ○
- ○
- ○

NOTES

THURSDAY: _____
HEART CHAKRA:

TO-DO

AFFIRMATION

SCHEDULE

APPOINTMENTS

TO-DO

MOOD

THURSDAY:

HEART CHAKRA:

AFFIRMATION:

GOALS	AM	PM	MEALS
○			BREAKFAST
			LUNCH
○			DINNER
			SNACKS
○			WATER 💧💧💧💧💧💧💧💧
			EXERCISE

GRATITUDE	TO DO	NOTES
	○ _____	
	○ _____	
	○ _____	
	○ _____	
	○ _____	
	○ _____	
CHAKRA CARE	○ _____	
	○ _____	
	○ _____	
	○ _____	

FRIDAY:

THROAT CHAKRA:

TO-DO

_____
_____
_____
_____

SCHEDULE

_____
_____
_____
_____
_____
_____
_____
_____
_____
_____
_____
_____
_____
_____
_____
_____
_____
_____

AFFIRMATION

APPOINTMENTS

TO-DO

- _____
- _____
- _____
- _____
- _____
- _____
- _____
- _____
- _____
- _____
- _____

MOOD

FRIDAY: _____

THROAT CHAKRA:

AFFIRMATION:

GOALS	AM	PM	MEALS
○ ○ ○			BREKFAST ──────── LUNCH ──────── DINNER ──────── SNACKS ──────── WATER 💧💧💧💧💧💧💧💧 EXERCISE

GRATITUDE	TO DO	NOTES
      CHAKRA CARE	○ ──────── ○ ──────── ○ ──────── ○ ──────── ○ ──────── ○ ──────── ○ ──────── ○ ──────── ○ ──────── ○ ────────	

SATURDAY:

3RD EYE CHAKRA:

TO-DO

AFFIRMATION

SCHEDULE

APPOINTMENTS

TO-DO

MOOD

SATURDAY:

3RD EYE CHAKRA:

AFFIRMATION:

GOALS	AM	PM	MEALS
○			BREAKFAST
○			LUNCH
			DINNER
○			SNACKS
			WATER 💧💧💧💧💧💧💧💧
			EXERCISE

GRATITUDE	TO DO	NOTES
	○	
	○	
	○	
	○	
	○	
	○	
CHAKRA CARE	○	
	○	
	○	

SUNDAY:

CROWN CHAKRA:

TO-DO

AFFIRMATION

SCHEDULE

APPOINTMENTS

TO-DO

MOOD

SUNDAY:

CROWN CHAKRA:

AFFIRMATION:

GOALS	AM	PM	MEALS
○			BREAKFAST
○			LUNCH
			DINNER
○			SNACKS
			WATER ○○○○○○○○○
			EXERCISE

GRATITUDE

TO DO
- ○ ___
- ○ ___
- ○ ___
- ○ ___
- ○ ___
- ○ ___
- ○ ___
- ○ ___
- ○ ___
- ○ ___

CHAKRA CARE

NOTES

WEEK OF: _____

MON	TUES
WED	THURS
FRI	SAT
SUN	NOTES

TO DO: _____

MON
- ○ _____
- ○ _____
- ○ _____
- ○ _____

TUES
- ○ _____
- ○ _____
- ○ _____
- ○ _____

WED
- ○ _____
- ○ _____
- ○ _____
- ○ _____

THURS
- ○ _____
- ○ _____
- ○ _____
- ○ _____

FRI
- ○ _____
- ○ _____
- ○ _____
- ○ _____

SAT
- ○ _____
- ○ _____
- ○ _____
- ○ _____

SUN
- ○ _____
- ○ _____
- ○ _____
- ○ _____

NOTES
- ○ _____
- ○ _____
- ○ _____
- ○ _____

1-MINUTE REFLECTIONS

MON	**TUES**

WED	**THURS**

FRI	**SAT**

SUN	**NOTES**

MONDAY:

ROOT CHAKRA:

TO-DO

AFFIRMATION

SCHEDULE

APPOINTMENTS

TO-DO

MOOD

MONDAY:

ROOT CHAKRA:

AFFIRMATION:

GOALS	AM	PM	MEALS
○			BREAKFAST
			LUNCH
○			DINNER
			SNACKS
○			WATER 💧💧💧💧💧💧💧💧
			EXERCISE

GRATITUDE	TO DO		NOTES
	○		
	○		
	○		
	○		
	○		
	○		
CHAKRA CARE	○		
	○		
	○		
	○		

TUESDAY:

SACRAL CHAKRA:

TO-DO

_____
_____
_____
_____

SCHEDULE

_____
_____
_____
_____
_____
_____
_____
_____
_____
_____
_____
_____
_____
_____
_____
_____
_____
_____

AFFIRMATION

APPOINTMENTS

TO-DO

☐ _____
☐ _____
☐ _____
☐ _____
☐ _____
☐ _____
☐ _____
☐ _____
☐ _____
☐ _____

MOOD

TUESDAY:

SACRAL CHAKRA:

AFFIRMATION:

GOALS	AM	PM	MEALS
○			BREAKFAST
			LUNCH
○			DINNER
			SNACKS
○			WATER 💧💧💧💧💧💧💧💧
			EXERCISE

GRATITUDE	TO DO	NOTES
	○	
	○	
	○	
	○	
	○	
	○	
CHAKRA CARE	○	
	○	
	○	
	○	

WEDNESDAY:

POWER CENTER:

TO-DO

SCHEDULE

AFFIRMATION

APPOINTMENTS

TO-DO

MOOD

WEDNESDAY:

POWER CENTER:

AFFIRMATION:

GOALS	AM	PM	MEALS
○			BREAKFAST
○			LUNCH
○			DINNER
			SNACKS
			WATER 💧💧💧💧💧💧💧💧
			EXERCISE

GRATITUDE

CHAKRA CARE

TO DO
- ○ _____
- ○ _____
- ○ _____
- ○ _____
- ○ _____
- ○ _____
- ○ _____
- ○ _____
- ○ _____
- ○ _____

NOTES

THURSDAY: _____

HEART CHAKRA:

TO-DO

_____
_____
_____
_____

SCHEDULE

_____
_____
_____
_____
_____
_____
_____
_____
_____
_____
_____
_____
_____
_____
_____
_____
_____
_____
_____

AFFIRMATION

APPOINTMENTS

TO-DO

- _____
- _____
- _____
- _____
- _____
- _____
- _____
- _____
- _____
- _____
- _____
- _____

MOOD

THURSDAY:

HEART CHAKRA:

AFFIRMATION:

GOALS	AM	PM	MEALS
○ ○ ○			BREAKFAST LUNCH DINNER SNACKS WATER 💧💧💧💧💧💧💧💧 EXERCISE

GRATITUDE	TO DO	NOTES
	○ ○ ○ ○ ○ ○ ○ ○ ○	
CHAKRA CARE		

FRIDAY:
THROAT CHAKRA:

TO-DO
_____
_____
_____
_____

SCHEDULE
_____
_____
_____
_____
_____
_____
_____
_____
_____
_____
_____
_____
_____
_____
_____
_____
_____
_____

AFFIRMATION

APPOINTMENTS

TO-DO
- _____
- _____
- _____
- _____
- _____
- _____
- _____
- _____
- _____
- _____

MOOD

FRIDAY: _____

THROAT CHAKRA:

AFFIRMATION:

GOALS	AM	PM	MEALS
○			BREAKFAST
○			LUNCH
○			DINNER
			SNACKS
			WATER 💧💧💧💧💧💧💧💧
			EXERCISE

GRATITUDE	TO DO	NOTES
	○	
	○	
	○	
	○	
	○	
	○	
CHAKRA CARE	○	
	○	
	○	
	○	

SATURDAY:

3RD EYE CHAKRA:

TO-DO

AFFIRMATION

SCHEDULE

APPOINTMENTS

TO-DO

MOOD

SATURDAY:

3RD EYE CHAKRA:

AFFIRMATION:

GOALS	AM	PM	MEALS
○			BREAKFAST
			LUNCH
○			DINNER
			SNACKS
○			WATER 💧💧💧💧💧💧💧💧💧💧
			EXERCISE

GRATITUDE	TO DO	NOTES
	○	
	○	
	○	
	○	
	○	
	○	
CHAKRA CARE	○	
	○	
	○	

SUNDAY:

CROWN CHAKRA:

TO-DO
_____
_____
_____
_____

SCHEDULE
_____
_____
_____
_____
_____
_____
_____
_____
_____
_____
_____
_____
_____
_____
_____

AFFIRMATION

APPOINTMENTS

TO-DO
- _____
- _____
- _____
- _____
- _____
- _____
- _____
- _____
- _____
- _____
- _____

MOOD

SUNDAY: _____

CROWN CHAKRA:

AFFIRMATION:

GOALS	AM	PM	MEALS
○			BREAKFAST
			LUNCH
○			DINNER
			SNACKS
○			WATER 💧💧💧💧💧💧💧💧
			EXERCISE

GRATITUDE	TO DO	NOTES
	○ _____	
	○ _____	
	○ _____	
	○ _____	
	○ _____	
	○ _____	
CHAKRA CARE	○ _____	
	○ _____	
	○ _____	
	○ _____	

WEEK OF: _____

MON	TUES

WED	THURS

FRI	SAT

SUN	NOTES

TO DO:

MON
- ○ _____
- ○ _____
- ○ _____
- ○ _____

TUES
- ○ _____
- ○ _____
- ○ _____
- ○ _____

WED
- ○ _____
- ○ _____
- ○ _____
- ○ _____

THURS
- ○ _____
- ○ _____
- ○ _____
- ○ _____

FRI
- ○ _____
- ○ _____
- ○ _____
- ○ _____

SAT
- ○ _____
- ○ _____
- ○ _____
- ○ _____

SUN
- ○ _____
- ○ _____
- ○ _____
- ○ _____

NOTES
- ○ _____
- ○ _____
- ○ _____
- ○ _____

1-MINUTE REFLECTIONS

MON

TUES

WED

THURS

FRI

SAT

SUN

NOTES

MONDAY:

ROOT CHAKRA:

TO-DO

_____
_____
_____
_____

SCHEDULE

_____
_____
_____
_____
_____
_____
_____
_____
_____
_____
_____
_____
_____
_____
_____
_____

AFFIRMATION

APPOINTMENTS

TO-DO

_____
_____
_____
_____
_____
_____
_____
_____
_____
_____

MOOD

MONDAY: _____

ROOT CHAKRA:

AFFIRMATION:

GOALS	AM	PM	MEALS
○ ○ ○			BREAKFAST LUNCH DINNER SNACKS WATER ○○○○○○○○ EXERCISE

GRATITUDE	TO DO	NOTES
	○ _____ ○ _____ ○ _____ ○ _____ ○ _____ ○ _____ ○ _____ ○ _____ ○ _____ ○ _____	
CHAKRA CARE		

TUESDAY:

SACRAL CHAKRA:

TO-DO

AFFIRMATION

SCHEDULE

APPOINTMENTS

TO-DO

MOOD

TUESDAY:

SACRAL CHAKRA:

AFFIRMATION:

GOALS	AM	PM	MEALS
○ ○ ○			BREAKFAST LUNCH DINNER SNACKS WATER 💧💧💧💧💧💧💧💧 EXERCISE

GRATITUDE

CHAKRA CARE

TO DO
- ○
- ○
- ○
- ○
- ○
- ○
- ○
- ○
- ○
- ○

NOTES

WEDNESDAY: _____

POWER CENTER:

TO-DO

_____
_____
_____

SCHEDULE

_____
_____
_____
_____
_____
_____
_____
_____
_____
_____
_____
_____
_____
_____
_____
_____
_____

AFFIRMATION

APPOINTMENTS

TO-DO

☐ _____
☐ _____
☐ _____
☐ _____
☐ _____
☐ _____
☐ _____
☐ _____
☐ _____
☐ _____
☐ _____
☐ _____

MOOD

WEDNESDAY:

POWER CENTER:

AFFIRMATION:

GOALS	AM	PM	MEALS
○			BREAKFAST
○			LUNCH
			DINNER
○			SNACKS
			WATER 💧💧💧💧💧💧💧💧
			EXERCISE

GRATITUDE

TO DO
- ○
- ○
- ○
- ○
- ○
- ○
- ○
- ○
- ○
- ○

CHAKRA CARE

NOTES

THURSDAY:

HEART CHAKRA:

TO-DO

_____
_____
_____
_____
_____

SCHEDULE

_____
_____
_____
_____
_____
_____
_____
_____
_____
_____
_____
_____
_____
_____
_____
_____
_____

AFFIRMATION

APPOINTMENTS

TO-DO

☐ _____
☐ _____
☐ _____
☐ _____
☐ _____
☐ _____
☐ _____
☐ _____
☐ _____
☐ _____
☐ _____
☐ _____

MOOD

THURSDAY:

HEART CHAKRA:

AFFIRMATION:

GOALS	AM	PM	MEALS
○ ○ ○			BREAKFAST LUNCH DINNER SNACKS WATER EXERCISE

GRATITUDE	TO DO	NOTES
CHAKRA CARE	○ ○ ○ ○ ○ ○ ○ ○ ○ ○	

FRIDAY:

THROAT CHAKRA:

TO-DO
_____
_____
_____
_____

SCHEDULE
_____
_____
_____
_____
_____
_____
_____
_____
_____
_____
_____
_____
_____
_____
_____
_____

AFFIRMATION

APPOINTMENTS

TO-DO
_____
_____
_____
_____
_____
_____
_____
_____
_____
_____

MOOD

FRIDAY:

THROAT CHAKRA:

AFFIRMATION:

GOALS	AM	PM	MEALS
○ ○ ○			BREAKFAST LUNCH DINNER SNACKS WATER 💧💧💧💧💧💧💧💧 EXERCISE

| GRATITUDE

 CHAKRA CARE | TO DO
 ○ ____
 ○ ____
 ○ ____
 ○ ____
 ○ ____
 ○ ____
 ○ ____
 ○ ____
 ○ ____
 ○ ____ | NOTES |

SATURDAY: _____

3RD EYE CHAKRA:

TO-DO

_____
_____
_____
_____

SCHEDULE

_____
_____
_____
_____
_____
_____
_____
_____
_____
_____
_____
_____
_____
_____
_____
_____
_____

AFFIRMATION

APPOINTMENTS

TO-DO

☐ _____
☐ _____
☐ _____
☐ _____
☐ _____
☐ _____
☐ _____
☐ _____
☐ _____
☐ _____

MOOD

SATURDAY:

3RD EYE CHAKRA:

AFFIRMATION:

GOALS	AM	PM	MEALS
○			BREAKFAST
○			LUNCH
○			DINNER
			SNACKS
			WATER 💧💧💧💧💧💧💧💧
			EXERCISE

GRATITUDE	TO DO	NOTES
	○	
	○	
	○	
	○	
	○	
	○	
CHAKRA CARE	○	
	○	
	○	
	○	

SUNDAY:

CROWN CHAKRA:

TO-DO
_____
_____
_____
_____

SCHEDULE
_____
_____
_____
_____
_____
_____
_____
_____
_____
_____
_____
_____
_____
_____
_____
_____
_____

AFFIRMATION

APPOINTMENTS

TO-DO
☐ _____
☐ _____
☐ _____
☐ _____
☐ _____
☐ _____
☐ _____
☐ _____
☐ _____
☐ _____

MOOD

SUNDAY:

CROWN CHAKRA:

AFFIRMATION:

GOALS	AM	PM	MEALS
○			BREAKFAST
			LUNCH
○			DINNER
			SNACKS
○			WATER ○○○○○○○○○○
			EXERCISE

GRATITUDE	TO DO	NOTES
	○	
	○	
	○	
	○	
	○	
	○	
CHAKRA CARE	○	
	○	
	○	
	○	

WEEK OF: _____

MON	TUES

WED	THURS

FRI	SAT

SUN	NOTES

TO DO:

MON

○ _____
○ _____
○ _____
○ _____

TUES

○ _____
○ _____
○ _____
○ _____

WED

○ _____
○ _____
○ _____
○ _____

THURS

○ _____
○ _____
○ _____
○ _____

FRI

○ _____
○ _____
○ _____
○ _____

SAT

○ _____
○ _____
○ _____
○ _____

SUN

○ _____
○ _____
○ _____
○ _____

NOTES

○ _____
○ _____
○ _____
○ _____

1-MINUTE REFLECTIONS

MON
_____
_____
_____
_____
_____

TUES
_____
_____
_____
_____
_____

WED
_____
_____
_____
_____
_____

THURS
_____
_____
_____
_____
_____

FRI
_____
_____
_____
_____
_____

SAT
_____
_____
_____
_____
_____

SUN
_____
_____
_____
_____
_____

NOTES
_____
_____
_____
_____
_____

MONDAY:

ROOT CHAKRA:

TO-DO
_____
_____
_____
_____

SCHEDULE
_____
_____
_____
_____
_____
_____
_____
_____
_____
_____
_____
_____
_____
_____

AFFIRMATION

APPOINTMENTS

TO-DO
- _____
- _____
- _____
- _____
- _____
- _____
- _____
- _____
- _____

MOOD

MONDAY: _____

ROOT CHAKRA:

AFFIRMATION:

GOALS	AM	PM	MEALS
○ ○ ○			BREAKFAST ___ LUNCH ___ DINNER ___ SNACKS ___ WATER 💧💧💧💧💧💧💧💧 EXERCISE ___

GRATITUDE	TO DO	NOTES
      CHAKRA CARE	○ ___ ○ ___ ○ ___ ○ ___ ○ ___ ○ ___ ○ ___ ○ ___ ○ ___ ○ ___	

TUESDAY:

SACRAL CHAKRA:

TO-DO

AFFIRMATION

SCHEDULE

APPOINTMENTS

TO-DO

MOOD

TUESDAY:

SACRAL CHAKRA:

AFFIRMATION:

GOALS	AM	PM	MEALS
○ ○ ○			BREAKFAST LUNCH DINNER SNACKS WATER 💧💧💧💧💧💧💧💧 EXERCISE

| GRATITUDE

 CHAKRA CARE | TO DO
 ○
 ○
 ○
 ○
 ○
 ○
 ○
 ○
 ○
 ○ | NOTES |

WEDNESDAY:

POWER CENTER:

TO-DO

SCHEDULE

AFFIRMATION

APPOINTMENTS

TO-DO

MOOD

WEDNESDAY:

POWER CENTER:

AFFIRMATION:

GOALS	AM	PM	MEALS
○ ○ ○			BREAKFAST / LUNCH / DINNER / SNACKS / WATER ○○○○○○○○ / EXERCISE

| GRATITUDE / CHAKRA CARE | TO DO ○ ○ ○ ○ ○ ○ ○ ○ ○ ○ | NOTES |

THURSDAY:
HEART CHAKRA:

TO-DO
_____
_____
_____
_____

SCHEDULE
_____
_____
_____
_____
_____
_____
_____
_____
_____
_____
_____
_____
_____
_____
_____
_____
_____
_____
_____
_____

AFFIRMATION

APPOINTMENTS

TO-DO
☐ _____
☐ _____
☐ _____
☐ _____
☐ _____
☐ _____
☐ _____
☐ _____
☐ _____
☐ _____
☐ _____
☐ _____

MOOD

THURSDAY:

HEART CHAKRA:

AFFIRMATION:

GOALS	AM	PM	MEALS
○			BREAKFAST
			LUNCH
○			DINNER
			SNACKS
○			WATER 💧💧💧💧💧💧💧💧
			EXERCISE

GRATITUDE	TO DO	NOTES
	○	
	○	
	○	
	○	
	○	
	○	
CHAKRA CARE	○	
	○	
	○	
	○	

FRIDAY:

THROAT CHAKRA:

TO-DO
_____
_____
_____
_____

SCHEDULE
_____
_____
_____
_____
_____
_____
_____
_____
_____
_____
_____
_____
_____
_____
_____
_____
_____
_____

AFFIRMATION

APPOINTMENTS

TO-DO
_____
_____
_____
_____
_____
_____
_____
_____
_____
_____
_____

MOOD

FRIDAY:

THROAT CHAKRA:

AFFIRMATION:

GOALS	AM	PM	MEALS
○			BREAKFAST
			LUNCH
○			DINNER
			SNACKS
○			WATER 💧💧💧💧💧💧💧💧
			EXERCISE

GRATITUDE / CHAKRA CARE	TO DO	NOTES
	○	
	○	
	○	
	○	
	○	
	○	
	○	
	○	
	○	
	○	

SATURDAY: _____

3RD EYE CHAKRA:

TO-DO
_____
_____
_____
_____

SCHEDULE
_____
_____
_____
_____
_____
_____
_____
_____
_____
_____
_____
_____
_____
_____
_____
_____
_____

AFFIRMATION

APPOINTMENTS

TO-DO
- _____
- _____
- _____
- _____
- _____
- _____
- _____
- _____
- _____
- _____

MOOD

SATURDAY: _____

3RD EYE CHAKRA:

AFFIRMATION:

GOALS	AM	PM	MEALS
○ ○ ○			BREAKFAST _____ LUNCH _____ DINNER _____ SNACKS _____ WATER 💧💧💧💧💧💧💧💧 EXERCISE

GRATITUDE	TO DO	NOTES
   CHAKRA CARE	○ _____ ○ _____ ○ _____ ○ _____ ○ _____ ○ _____ ○ _____ ○ _____ ○ _____ ○ _____	

SUNDAY:

CROWN CHAKRA:

TO-DO

SCHEDULE

AFFIRMATION

APPOINTMENTS

TO-DO

MOOD

SUNDAY:

CROWN CHAKRA:

AFFIRMATION:

GOALS	AM	PM	MEALS
○ ○ ○			BREAKFAST LUNCH DINNER SNACKS WATER 💧💧💧💧💧💧💧💧 EXERCISE

| GRATITUDE

 CHAKRA CARE | TO DO
 ○ _____
 ○ _____
 ○ _____
 ○ _____
 ○ _____
 ○ _____
 ○ _____
 ○ _____
 ○ _____
 ○ _____ | NOTES |

WEEK OF: _____

MON	TUES
WED	THURS
FRI	SAT
SUN	NOTES

TO DO: _____

MON
- ○ _____
- ○ _____
- ○ _____
- ○ _____

TUES
- ○ _____
- ○ _____
- ○ _____
- ○ _____

WED
- ○ _____
- ○ _____
- ○ _____
- ○ _____

THURS
- ○ _____
- ○ _____
- ○ _____
- ○ _____

FRI
- ○ _____
- ○ _____
- ○ _____
- ○ _____

SAT
- ○ _____
- ○ _____
- ○ _____
- ○ _____

SUN
- ○ _____
- ○ _____
- ○ _____
- ○ _____

NOTES
- ○ _____
- ○ _____
- ○ _____
- ○ _____

1-MINUTE REFLECTIONS

MON

TUES

WED

THURS

FRI

SAT

SUN

NOTES

MONDAY:

ROOT CHAKRA:

TO-DO

_____
_____
_____
_____

SCHEDULE

_____
_____
_____
_____
_____
_____
_____
_____
_____
_____
_____
_____
_____
_____
_____
_____
_____
_____
_____

AFFIRMATION

APPOINTMENTS

TO-DO

- _____
- _____
- _____
- _____
- _____
- _____
- _____
- _____
- _____
- _____
- _____
- _____

MOOD

MONDAY: _____

ROOT CHAKRA:

AFFIRMATION:

GOALS	AM	PM	MEALS
○			BREAKFAST
			LUNCH
○			DINNER
			SNACKS
○			WATER 💧💧💧💧💧💧💧💧
			EXERCISE

GRATITUDE	TO DO	NOTES
	○ _____	
	○ _____	
	○ _____	
	○ _____	
	○ _____	
	○ _____	
CHAKRA CARE	○ _____	
	○ _____	
	○ _____	
	○ _____	

TUESDAY: _____

SACRAL CHAKRA:

TO-DO

_____
_____
_____
_____

SCHEDULE

_____
_____
_____
_____
_____
_____
_____
_____
_____
_____
_____
_____
_____
_____
_____
_____
_____

AFFIRMATION

APPOINTMENTS

TO-DO

☐ _____
☐ _____
☐ _____
☐ _____
☐ _____
☐ _____
☐ _____
☐ _____
☐ _____
☐ _____
☐ _____

MOOD

TUESDAY:

SACRAL CHAKRA:

AFFIRMATION:

GOALS	AM	PM	MEALS
○ ○ ○			BREAKFAST LUNCH DINNER SNACKS WATER 💧💧💧💧💧💧💧💧 EXERCISE

GRATITUDE CHAKRA CARE	TO DO ○ _____ ○ _____ ○ _____ ○ _____ ○ _____ ○ _____ ○ _____ ○ _____ ○ _____ ○ _____	NOTES

WEDNESDAY:

POWER CENTER:

TO-DO

SCHEDULE

AFFIRMATION

APPOINTMENTS

TO-DO

MOOD

WEDNESDAY:

POWER CENTER:

AFFIRMATION:

GOALS	AM	PM	MEALS
○ ○ ○			BREAKFAST LUNCH DINNER SNACKS WATER 💧💧💧💧💧💧💧💧 EXERCISE

GRATITUDE	TO DO	NOTES
     CHAKRA CARE	○ _____ ○ _____ ○ _____ ○ _____ ○ _____ ○ _____ ○ _____ ○ _____ ○ _____ ○ _____	

THURSDAY: _____

HEART CHAKRA:

TO-DO
_____
_____
_____
_____

SCHEDULE
_____
_____
_____
_____
_____
_____
_____
_____
_____
_____
_____
_____
_____
_____
_____
_____
_____
_____

AFFIRMATION

APPOINTMENTS

TO-DO
- _____
- _____
- _____
- _____
- _____
- _____
- _____
- _____
- _____
- _____
- _____

MOOD

THURSDAY:

HEART CHAKRA:

AFFIRMATION:

GOALS	AM	PM	MEALS
○			BREAKFAST
			LUNCH
○			DINNER
			SNACKS
○			WATER 💧💧💧💧💧💧💧💧
			EXERCISE

GRATITUDE	TO DO	NOTES
	○	
	○	
	○	
	○	
	○	
	○	
CHAKRA CARE	○	
	○	
	○	
	○	

FRIDAY:

THROAT CHAKRA:

TO-DO
_____
_____
_____
_____
_____

SCHEDULE
_____
_____
_____
_____
_____
_____
_____
_____
_____
_____
_____
_____
_____
_____
_____
_____
_____
_____

AFFIRMATION

APPOINTMENTS

TO-DO
_____
_____
_____
_____
_____
_____
_____
_____
_____
_____
_____
_____

MOOD

FRIDAY:

THROAT CHAKRA:

AFFIRMATION:

GOALS	AM	PM	MEALS
○ ○ ○			BREAKFAST LUNCH DINNER SNACKS WATER 💧💧💧💧💧💧💧💧 EXERCISE

GRATITUDE

CHAKRA CARE

TO DO
- ○
- ○
- ○
- ○
- ○
- ○
- ○
- ○
- ○
- ○

NOTES

SATURDAY:

3RD EYE CHAKRA:

TO-DO

AFFIRMATION

APPOINTMENTS

SCHEDULE

TO-DO

MOOD

SATURDAY: _____

3RD EYE CHAKRA:

AFFIRMATION:

GOALS	AM	PM	MEALS
○ ○ ○			BREAKFAST _____ LUNCH _____ DINNER _____ SNACKS _____ WATER 💧💧💧💧💧💧💧💧 EXERCISE _____
GRATITUDE **CHAKRA CARE**	**TO DO** ○ _____ ○ _____ ○ _____ ○ _____ ○ _____ ○ _____ ○ _____ ○ _____ ○ _____ ○ _____	**NOTES**	

SUNDAY:

CROWN CHAKRA:

TO-DO

_____
_____
_____
_____
_____

SCHEDULE

_____
_____
_____
_____
_____
_____
_____
_____
_____
_____
_____
_____
_____
_____
_____
_____
_____
_____
_____

AFFIRMATION

APPOINTMENTS

TO-DO

- _____
- _____
- _____
- _____
- _____
- _____
- _____
- _____
- _____
- _____
- _____
- _____

MOOD

SUNDAY:

CROWN CHAKRA:

AFFIRMATION:

GOALS	AM	PM	MEALS
○			BREAKFAST
			LUNCH
○			DINNER
			SNACKS
○			WATER 💧💧💧💧💧💧💧💧
			EXERCISE

GRATITUDE	TO DO	NOTES
	○	
	○	
	○	
	○	
	○	
	○	
CHAKRA CARE	○	
	○	
	○	
	○	

NOTES

NOTES

NOTES

NOTES

NOTES